Contents

DID YOU KNOW? Discover amazing facts about heat.

THE SCIENCE OF HEAT Find out more about the science of heat and heat energy.

HEAT FIRSTS Learn more about heat inventions and discoveries.

1ST

Some words are shown in bold, **like this**. You can find out what they mean by looking in the glossary.

The journey of heat

Heat *is a form of* **energy**. *It is one of many different forms of energy. Every action or activity uses energy by changing it from one form to another. A torch or flashlight changes electrical energy into light. An electric motor changes electrical energy into movement. A radio changes electrical energy into sound.*

▲ The heat energy in a hot drink warms the cup and flows out into its surroundings – and into you if you take a sip!

Heat always flows from hot to cold. If you drop an ice cube into a glass of water, heat flows from the water into the colder ice cube. The water cools down and the ice cube warms up. As the ice warms up, it melts.

Did you Know?
Temperature and heat are not the same. Imagine an **iceberg** and a cup of boiling water. Boiling water has a higher temperature than ice, but the iceberg has more heat! Confused? The iceberg contains millions of cups of frozen water. Each one has a little bit of heat energy. Multiplied by millions, the whole iceberg has more heat energy than one cup of boiling water.

Crude oil to fast food

Fast food is called fast food because it needs very little preparation, or none at all, before it is ready to be eaten. It couldn't be made without heat. The journey of heat in this book begins with **crude oil**. The energy the oil contains will be changed into all sorts of different forms of energy on its long journey to a fast-food snack.

THE SCIENCE OF HEAT

Have you ever wondered what heat is? If you could see the particles of matter that everything is made of, you would see that they are shaking. The particles, called **atoms**, vibrate. The hotter something is, the more the atoms vibrate. And that is all heat is – vibrating atoms.

▲ Everything, even an iceberg, contains heat energy.

Where does oil come from?

Our energy journey really began millions of years ago. Crude oil started off as microscopic plants and creatures called plankton that lived in the ocean. When they died, they sank to the seabed and became buried under mud. Over millions of years, heat from inside Earth and the huge weight of mud pressing down on them changed them into oil. **Natural gas** *often collected above the oil.*

The same happened on land. When plants growing on swampy land died, they became buried under soil, trapping the energy they received from the Sun. Over millions of years, heat and pressure changed them into coal.

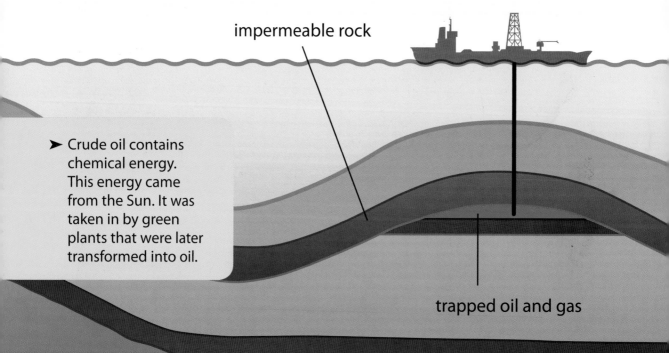

impermeable rock

➤ Crude oil contains chemical energy. This energy came from the Sun. It was taken in by green plants that were later transformed into oil.

trapped oil and gas

Rock sponge

By the time oil formed, the mud above it had become rock. The sandy rock soaked up the oil like a sponge. Thick layers of **impermeable** rock trapped the oil underneath them. Over millions of years, the ground was worn away by wind and rain. Sometimes, this brought oil up to the surface, but it is usually found much deeper underground.

About 100 countries produce crude oil. The top five are Saudi Arabia, Russia, the United States, China and Canada. The oil isn't the same everywhere. In some places it is a runny oil called light crude. In other places the oil that comes out of the ground is a much thicker oil called heavy crude.

▲ Crude oil is so close to the ground surface in some places that it seeps out, forming oily black pools.

Drilling for oil

Oil is brought to the surface by drilling a hole down through the ground to reach it. The deepest oil wells in production today lie more than 10,600 metres (35,000 feet) underground. When the drill reaches the oil, the weight of rock pressing down above it forces the oil up to the surface. Years later, when the flow of oil begins to weaken, water or gas can be pumped down into the rock to force more oil out.

▲ A diamond-tipped drill cuts through the rock to reach the oil.

Offshore oil

A lot of oil formed in seabed rock which still lies deep underwater today. **Drilling rigs** in the sea drill down into these oil fields. If oil or gas is found, the exploration rig moves away and a production platform is brought in to bring up the oil or gas. Some **offshore** platforms sit on the seabed. In deeper water, floating platforms are used. These offshore platforms can work in water up to about 3,000 metres (10,000 feet) deep.

▲ Offshore drilling platforms are massive structures. The biggest and heaviest weigh more than 1 million tonnes (1.1 million tons).

DID YOU KNOW?

Oil wells have been drilled since ancient times. **Bamboo** drills were used in China more than 1,600 years ago. The oil well that started the modern oil industry was drilled in Titusville, Pennsylvania, USA, in 1859. Local people laughed at the idea of drilling for oil. But when oil was found, people flocked to the area to drill their own wells and make their fortunes.

Making oil useful

Crude oil isn't very useful. It doesn't burn easily. It is changed into more useful **fuels** and other substances by using heat. This is done in chemical plants called **refineries**.

▲ Oil is transported to refineries by giant tanker ships. More than 2 billion tonnes of oil and products made from oil are transported by sea every year.

The crude oil is heated and pumped into a tall tower. The tower is hot at the bottom and cooler higher up. The heat boils the oil and makes some of it **evaporate** (change to gas). The gas rises up the tower. As it cools down, some of it changes back to liquid. Different liquids form at different heights in the tower. Using heat like this is called fractional distillation. It changes crude oil into more useful fuels, oils, gases, waxes and chemicals. A thick tar-like material called bitumen or asphalt is left at the bottom of the tower. This is used for making roads.

Fuel for food

Oil and other fuels are used to provide some of the energy needed by the food industry. They might be burned to provide heat, or they might be burned in truck engines transporting food, or they might be burned in power stations to make electricity.

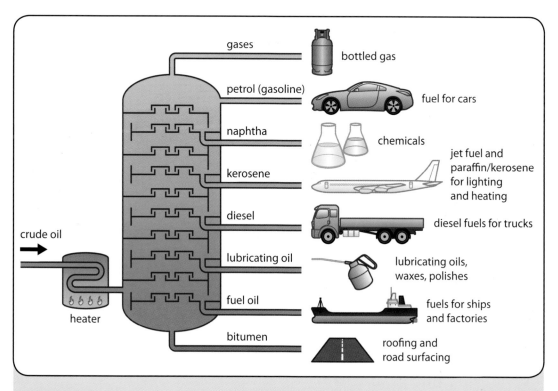

▲ A distillation tower splits crude oil up into more useful materials.

Crude oil is transported to refineries by giant ships called oil tankers. The biggest tanker ships are called Ultra Large Crude Carriers (ULCCs). Each of these giant ships is 380 metres (1,247 feet) long – longer than three football fields. Fully loaded, they can weigh more than 500,000 tonnes (550,000 tons). They can each carry 500 million litres (132 million US gallons) of oil or oil products.

How is oil used in the food industry?

Fuel made in oil refineries powers the engines of all the trucks, ships and planes that transport goods all over the world. Their cargoes include meat, vegetables, fruit, grain, flour and other foodstuffs being transported from farms to food producers.

➤ The trucks that carry food materials to food processing plants and bakeries are powered by engines burning diesel oil, another fuel made from crude oil.

Fuel contains chemical energy. The energy is released by burning the fuel to change its chemical energy into heat energy. The heat makes air inside a truck's engine or a ship's engine expand (grow bigger). The force of the expanding air makes the engine turn the truck's wheels or the ship's propellers. The heat then escapes from the engine into the surrounding air.

Keeping food fresh

Some food ingredients spoil or rot in a short time. If they have to be transported long distances, they are often sent quickly by air. Another way to transport them is to pack them into **refrigerated** containers. The cold containers stop the food from spoiling so quickly. When they reach their destination, they are loaded onto trucks for the last part of their journey.

▲ Food that spoils quickly can be transported halfway around the world by air within a few hours.

▲ Power stations, like this one, convert energy from coal, oil or natural gas into electricity.

Making electricity

Some of the fuel made from crude oil is used to make electricity, and some of the electricity is used to make fast-food snacks. The oil, or another fuel such as coal or natural gas, is burned in a power station to heat water and change it into steam. The steam spins a **turbine**, and the turbine powers an electricity **generator**.

THE SCIENCE OF HEAT))))

Burning is one way to produce heat. This is also called combustion. It is a chemical reaction between a fuel and, usually, oxygen. The chemical reaction gives out energy in the form of heat and light. The heat makes gas produced by the chemical reaction glow. And that is what flames are – gas so hot that it glows.

Heat to movement

Burning converts the chemical energy in the oil or another fuel into heat energy. Then it changes into the **kinetic energy** (movement) of the steam. The steam passes this on to the turbine and then the generator changes it into electrical energy. The electricity can then be used to power all sorts of devices and machines in the factories and processing plants that make fast-food snacks.

Did you know?

About a third of the energy used all over the world comes from oil. Most of it is used for heating or for powering engines. Some electricity is also made from oil, but most electricity is made by burning other fuels such as coal or natural gas.

▲ Small electricity generators, like this one, make electricity by burning fuel made from crude oil.

Heating glasshouses

Electricity generated from oil and other fuels heats glasshouses and greenhouses across the world. Here, some salad crops such as lettuce and tomatoes are grown for use in burgers and sandwiches.

HEAT FIRSTS

1ST

Greenhouses have been used to grow food plants since Roman times, about 2,000 years ago. Before flat glass could be made, the first greenhouses were glazed with mica, a material that can be split into very thin sheets. The first known greenhouse was made for the Roman emperor Tiberius. Called a specularium, it was used to grow cucumber-like fruit for the emperor.

▲ Heated greenhouses provide the best conditions to grow tomatoes and other salad plants, whatever the weather is like outside.

Glasshouses are warm inside because they trap heat from the Sun. But if they aren't hot enough, especially at night, electric heaters boost the temperature even higher. The heaters change electrical energy into heat energy. Fans change electrical energy into kinetic energy to blow the warm air through the glasshouse.

Windows and blinds

In some glasshouses, motors convert electrical energy into kinetic energy to open and close windows, or open and close blinds, to keep the glasshouse at exactly the right temperature.

THE SCIENCE OF HEAT))))

Heat travels from place to place in three ways. One of them is **convection**. (The other two are **conduction** and **radiation**.) Hot air is lighter than cold air, and so it rises. When part of a glasshouse or a room is heated, the warm air rises and carries the heat to other parts.

▲ So much land in Spain is covered with greenhouses that they can be seen from space and look like a vast shimmering mirror stretched across the ground.

Machine energy

Some of the electricity made from oil and other fuels is used to make fast food. The machines in a food-processing plant work by converting electrical energy into other forms of energy. There are mixers to combine ingredients and conveyor belts to move food from one machine to another. The ovens that cook the food convert electrical energy into heat.

▲ A food-processing factory is a huge energy converter. It converts electrical energy into different forms of energy to run the machines.

THE SCIENCE OF HEAT

Conduction is the second of the three ways in which heat travels. Imagine a cooking pot sitting on a stove. Atoms vibrating in the hot stove make atoms in the pot vibrate, so the pot heats up. The vibrations spread to the food in the pot, so the food heats up, too. Things have to be touching each other for heat to travel through them by conduction.

Movement, heat, and noise

In the biggest factories, some of the work is done by electrically powered robots. There are also machines that fill packets, pots, bags and trays with food. They convert electrical energy into kinetic energy. All the machines warm up after they have been working for a while, and some of them are noisy, so some of their energy is being changed into heat and sound, too.

The food for fast-food snacks has been grown, harvested, transported, processed and cooked. But why is food cooked and what does cooking do to it?

▲ The human workers in food-processing factories are energy converters, too. They convert chemical energy in their muscles into kinetic energy.

What does cooking do to food?

Cooking changes food in a number of ways. Heat changes its flavour, **texture** *and colour. One of the most important things cooking does is to kill* **bacteria** *(germs) and other organisms that might cause all sorts of illnesses and diseases. Some bacteria can grow and multiply at temperatures of up to 60 degrees Celsius (140 degrees Fahrenheit). Food has to be heated to a higher temperature than this during cooking to kill all the bacteria and make sure the food is safe to eat.*

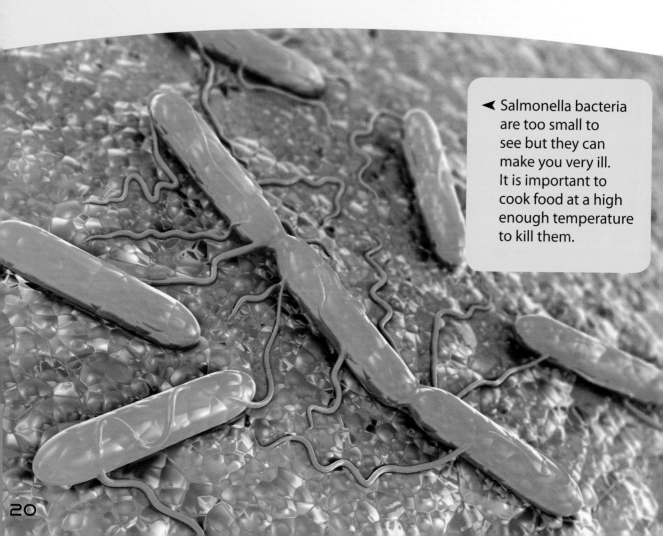

◄ Salmonella bacteria are too small to see but they can make you very ill. It is important to cook food at a high enough temperature to kill them.

Releasing goodness

Cooking softens vegetables. It usually makes all sorts of foods taste better, too. It makes meat juicier. It also releases **minerals**, **vitamins** and **nutrients** from food that the body can take in and use.

Some scientists think that our distant ancestors' ability to use fire to cook food enabled them to grow bigger brains and become modern humans. Cooking food makes it easier for us to **absorb** its energy. And we used the extra energy to grow bigger brains.

➤ Our distant ancestors started using fire to cook food at least a million years ago.

THE SCIENCE OF HEAT

Radiation is the third way in which heat travels. (The other two are conduction and convection.) Heat energy travels through space as waves, like light and radio waves. The only difference between heat, light and radio waves is their length. Heat waves are longer than light waves and shorter than radio waves. They are all energy waves called electromagnetic waves.

CONDUCTION, CONVECTION AND RADIATION

Heat travels from place to place in three ways – conduction, convection and radiation. You can find out more about them by doing this simple experiment with some spoons.

You will need:
- **metal spoon**
- **three plastic spoons**
- **mug of warm water**
- **modeling clay.**

Making it work

1 Pour some warm (not boiling) water into a mug.

2 Put a metal spoon and a plastic spoon in the mug and count to 10.

3 Take each spoon out and feel it to see which spoon is warmer.

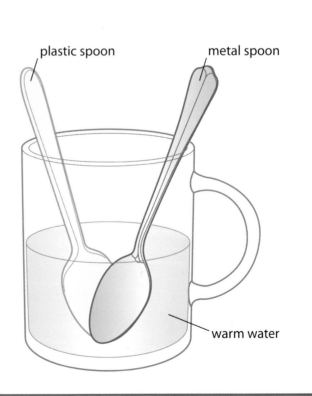

plastic spoon

metal spoon

warm water

4 Now take three plastic spoons. Stand one in a mug of warm water. Lay the second one across the top of the mug, and stand the third one a thumb's width away from the mug. Use a piece of modelling clay to make it stand upright.

plastic spoons

5 After five minutes, pick up each spoon and feel how warm it is.

What happened?

In the first part of the experiment, the two spoons in the water are heated by conduction. You should find that the metal spoon feels warmer than the plastic spoon. This is because metal conducts heat better and faster than plastic, so it heats up faster. This is why cooking pots and pans are made of metal. Heat passes through them quickly and starts cooking the food inside.

In the second part of the experiment, the spoon in the warm water is heated by conduction, because it touches the water. You'll probably find that this spoon is the warmest. The spoon on top of the mug is heated by convection – warm air currents rising from the water. You'll probably find that it is warm but not as warm as the spoon in the water. And the third spoon is heated by radiation. You'll probably find that this has been heated the least, because a mug of warm water radiates very little heat.

Heat from cookers

When an electric hob is turned on, it changes electrical energy into heat. The heat travels through pots and pans sitting on top of the cooker, and heats the food inside them. Food cooked inside an oven is heated by convection and radiation. Then the heat starts to change the food.

Cooking meat

Meat is the muscle of an animal. It is made of bundles of fibres. The fibres shorten when the muscle tightens and lengthen again when the muscle relaxes. The fibres are made of long **molecules** called proteins.

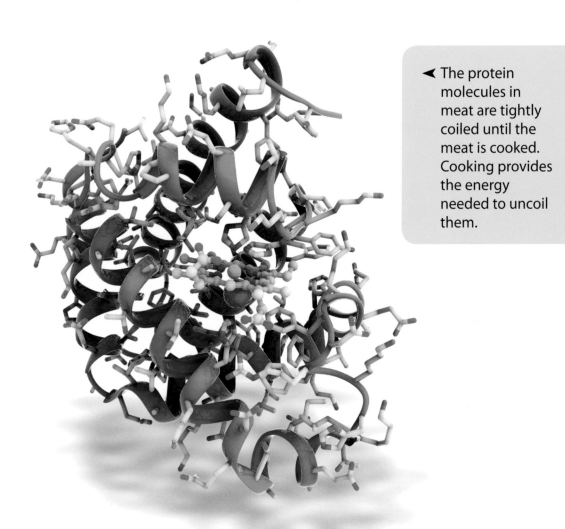

◄ The protein molecules in meat are tightly coiled until the meat is cooked. Cooking provides the energy needed to uncoil them.

In raw meat, the proteins are coiled up like jumbled pieces of string. When meat is cooked, heat makes the coils of protein unwind and join together. The muscle fibres shrink, forcing water out of them. It is important to get the cooking time right as well as the temperature. If cooking goes on for too long, too much liquid is forced out and the meat becomes dry and tough to eat.

THE SCIENCE OF HEAT

If you crack open a raw egg, the egg white is clear and gloopy. When it is heated, it changes in the same way as meat. Protein molecules in the egg white unwind and join together. When they join together, they do it in a way that stops light from passing through, so the clear, gloopy egg white changes into a white solid.

▲ Meat and eggs look different, but they both contain protein, so heat changes them in the same way.

Baking bread

Bread is an important part of fast food, including burgers and sandwiches. A burger needs a bread roll. Sandwiches need slices of bread. Bread is made from a stretchy mixture of flour and water called dough. When yeast is added to the dough, it produces a gas called carbon dioxide. This forms small bubbles in the dough, making the dough rise.

▲ Bread is light and fluffy because it is full of air spaces.

When the dough is baked in an oven, the heat of the oven changes it. Heat makes gas expand, so the bubbles in the dough grow bigger. Heat also changes the dough itself. The stretchy dough hardens. The heavy, wet dough is transformed into light, fluffy bread.

Popping corn

Another fast-food snack, popcorn, depends on the effect of heat, too. The corn starts off tooth-breakingly hard. When it is heated, moisture inside the corn changes to steam. Steam takes up much more space than water, so the pressure inside the corn rises until the hard shell gives way and bursts. The starch inside the corn is blown out. It instantly becomes a soft, air-filled **foam** that quickly cools and sets.

When fast-food snacks have been made and cooked, they then have to be packaged. Oil and heat play an important part in this.

Did You Know?

People were grinding grain to make flour for breadmaking at least 30,000 years ago. Archaeologists have found starch grains on ancient grinding stones. The ground-up starch from plant roots would have been cooked to make a flat bread like a hard pancake.

▲ Heat transforms rock-hard corn into soft, fluffy popcorn.

How is food packaged?

Some of the crude oil at the beginning of our energy journey is used to make packaging for food. Fast food is often packaged in plastic boxes, trays and wrappers. Plastic is used because it can be moulded into almost any shape of container or tray. Some of the packaging may be clear plastic film. This seals the food in, keeps bacteria out and lets customers see the food inside. Plastic is made from crude oil.

➤ Plastic packaging helps to keep hot food hot and frozen food frozen.

HEAT FIRSTS

1ST

Temperature is measured by thermometers. The first thermometers were made about 400 years ago, but they all used different temperature scales. A temperature measured by a thermometer is meaningless unless everyone agrees to use the same temperature scale. In the 1700s, the German scientist Daniel Gabriel Fahrenheit and the Swedish astronomer Anders Celsius invented temperature scales that were named after them and are still used today.

Making plastic

Plastic is made of long chain-like molecules called hydrocarbons, that are found in oil. By adding oxygen, sulphur, nitrogen or chlorine to hydrocarbons, scientists can make different types of plastic, including nylon, PVC and polythene. Some plastics are stiff and others are flexible. Some melt when they are heated, while others stay hard.

DID YOU KNOW?

Fast-food snacks that are sold hot are often packaged in a plastic called expanded polystyrene (EPS). This is a hard plastic that contains a lot of air bubbles. Air and plastic are both poor **conductors** of heat. The plastic foam stops heat escaping from the food. This keeps the food hot while the packaging stays cool enough to hold.

▲ This magnified image of expanded polystyrene shows the many air bubbles it contains.

Stopping the rot

Fast-food snacks that will be stored for some time before they are eaten are **preserved** to make them last longer. One common way to preserve food is to take away some of the heat energy it contains by cooling it down in a fridge or freezer. Chilly temperatures slow down the growth of germs and mould that would spoil the food and make it dangerous to eat.

▲ Pizzas are often preserved by freezing. After a few minutes in a hot oven they're ready to eat.

Some foods aren't frozen, because freezing harms them. Plants are made of cells full of water. When a plant freezes, ice crystals form inside the cells. As the crystals grow, they burst the cells. When the food is warmed up, the cells collapse like a pile of burst balloons and the food turns to mush. For this reason, watery foods such as tomatoes, cucumbers and strawberries are not preserved by freezing.

Drying out

Another way to preserve food is to take all the water out of it, because germs and mould need water to grow. Drying out food like this is called **dehydration**. As well as preserving the food, the dried-out food is very light and easy to transport.

THE SCIENCE OF HEAT

Food is sometimes dried, or dehydrated, by a process called freeze-drying. First, the food is frozen solid in a freezer. Then the frozen food is placed in an airtight tank and all the air is sucked out. The ice changes to gas without melting first. This is called sublimation.

▲ Freeze-drying works well with some types of fruit and it is sometimes used to make instant coffee granules.

PRESERVING FOOD

Investigate the effect of refrigeration on food.

You will need:
- **two slices of bread**
- **two paper plates**
- **two clear plastic bags.**

Making it work

1 Put a slice of bread on each paper plate and put them to one side for a couple of hours.

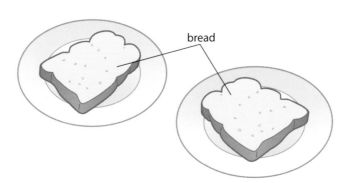

bread

2 Then put each slice of bread inside a plastic bag.

3 Put one plate on a windowsill and the second plate in a fridge.

4 Check the bread every day and look for changes. You'll probably find that the bread on the windowsill changes first. Blue patches of mould will appear on it.

What happened?

Even in a clean house, there are mould spores in the air. Some of them land on both slices of bread before they are put into the plastic bags. The bread contains some moisture that helps the spores to grow.

The bread in the fridge doesn't go mouldy as quickly as the other bread, because the low temperature in the fridge slows down all biological activity. Mould takes longer to grow there. This shows that taking heat out of food keeps food fresh for longer.

SAFETY FIRST

At the end of the experiment, throw the paper plates, bread and plastic bags away safely in a bin and then wash your hands with soap and water.

Doing the impossible

Fridges have to make heat travel from the cold air inside them to the warmer air outside. But doesn't heat always travel from hot to cold? So how do fridges work?

Before there were electric fridges, people used cold streams, ice and snow to preserve food by keeping it cold. Ships collected ice from lakes in Canada and Scandinavia and took it to warmer countries. People used the ice to line food cabinets and keep them cold.

▲ Before electric fridges, some wealthy people kept their food cold in ice-houses like this.

Liquid to gas

A liquid that evaporates at a very low temperature is piped into a fridge. It needs energy to evaporate. It takes this energy from inside the fridge in the form of heat, changing the liquid into a gas. The gas is piped out of the fridge and squashed. Squashing it changes it back to a liquid. When it changes to liquid it gives out the heat it collected from the fridge. The heat escapes and warms the surrounding air. The cool liquid is then pumped back inside the fridge, where it evaporates again and absorbs more heat.

When fast-food snacks have been prepared, packaged and delivered to shops, they are ready to be bought and eaten. Some of them need to be heated, using energy from crude oil and other fuels.

▲ The heat taken from inside a fridge to cool it down has to go somewhere. This is why the back of a fridge or freezer feels warm.

THE SCIENCE OF HEAT

The coldest possible temperature is called **absolute zero**. When something is cooled down, its atoms vibrate less and less. If the temperature keeps falling, the atoms will stop vibrating altogether. Nothing can be colder than this. The coldest possible temperature, absolute zero, is -273.15 degrees Celsius (-459.67 degrees Fahrenheit).

How is fast food prepared?

Fast food needs very little preparation by us, or none at all. Sandwiches and hot food just have to be unwrapped. Other fast foods need extra heat energy to warm them up.

Re-heating food

Some fast food is cooked in the factory where it is made and then quickly chilled or frozen. At home, the heat energy is put back into the food to make it ready for eating. The fastest way to heat ready-cooked fast food is to use a **microwave** oven. It changes electrical energy into microwaves and heats food by firing the microwaves at it.

HEAT FIRSTS   1ST

When Percy Spencer was working on **radar** equipment in 1945, he found that chocolate in his pocket had melted. Microwaves coming from the radar equipment had heated the chocolate. Spencer found that he could heat food by aiming microwaves at it. He had invented the microwave oven.

NOODLES

▲ Hot water transforms dehydrated (dried) food into a tasty snack.

The plastic film covering a fast-food tray usually has to be pierced before the food is heated, because heat makes the gas inside the tray expand. Without holes in the plastic film, the package might burst.

THE SCIENCE OF HEAT

A microwave oven works by using invisible waves called microwaves. Microwaves have **electromagnetic energy**, the same energy that is carried by light and radio waves. Microwaves are longer than light waves and shorter than radio waves. When microwaves hit food, the food absorbs their energy and changes it into heat. Then the heat spreads through the food by conduction.

▲ A microwave oven uses electromagnetic energy to heat food.

UNDER PRESSURE

You can see the effect of heat on gas by doing this simple experiment with a plastic bottle.

You will need:
- **an empty plastic soft-drink bottle – a 2-litre (half US gallon) bottle works well**
- **a party balloon.**

Making it work

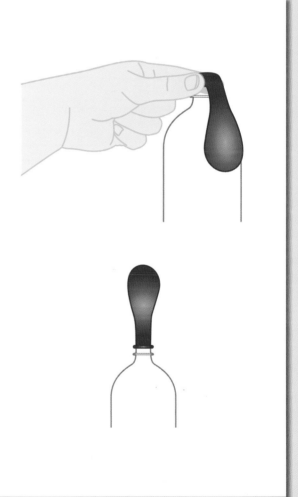

1 Take off the bottle's top and place the bottle in a fridge overnight to cool it and the air inside it.

2 Next day, take the bottle out of the fridge and quickly stretch a party balloon over its neck so that the balloon is empty and hangs down the side of the bottle.

3 Now stand the bottle on a flat surface and watch. The balloon quickly inflates and stands straight up on top of the bottle.

4 Now place the bottle, with the balloon still attached to it, back in the fridge. Check it a few minutes later and you should find that the balloon has collapsed again.

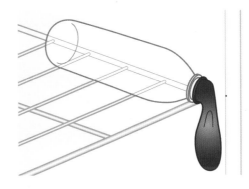

5 Now place the bottle in a freezer. Check it a few minutes later. You should find that the balloon has collapsed even more. It might even have been sucked inside the bottle.

6 If you leave the bottle in the freezer and check it again later, you might find that the bottle itself has started to collapse, as if someone is squashing it.

What happened?

When you take the bottle out of the fridge, the air inside it is very cold. It quickly starts warming up. As the air inside the bottle warms up, it expands. The expanding air fills the balloon and makes it stand up.

When you place the bottle back in the fridge, the air inside it contracts again. There isn't enough air to blow up the balloon, so the balloon collapses. When you put the bottle in a freezer, the air inside the bottle continues to cool down and contracts even more. The surrounding air squashes the bottle.

Body heat

The chemical energy and heat energy stored in a fast-food snack are absorbed by your body. Inside your body, the food is broken down by chemical reactions to release its energy.

You body uses the energy from food for growth and movement. Some of the energy from the food keeps you warm. All warm objects, including the human body, radiate (give out) heat. Your body radiates as much energy as a 100-watt lightbulb.

▲ The colours in this picture of a human body show temperature. White and red are the hottest, where the body is radiating the most heat.

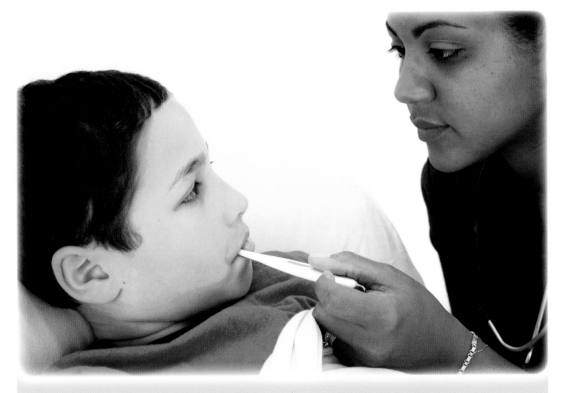

▲ A change in body temperature is one sign that you might be unwell.

An energy journey

So, think about the heat that helped to form crude oil deep underground. Millions of years later, it helped to make a fast-food snack, and has now become heat radiated by the person who ate the snack.

On its long journey, this heat changed into many different forms of energy, including chemical energy, electrical energy and kinetic energy. And it will continue changing from one form of energy to another in the future.

Did You Know? Your body is able to control its temperature without you having to think about it. Your hands and nose might be cold on a chilly winter's day and you might be sweating on a hot summer's day, but the temperature inside your body stays the same. The temperature of a healthy person is about 36.8 degrees Celsius (98.6 degrees Fahrenheit).

What have we learned about heat?

After following heat all the way from crude oil to a fast-food snack, we have learned the following about heat:

▲ Cooked fast food is often kept hot under lamps that radiate heat on to it.

- Heat is a form of energy.
- It is caused by the vibrations and movement of atoms.
- Energy is the ability to do work, so heat can do work.
- Heat can be converted (changed) into other forms of energy.
- It can make a gas expand (spread out more).
- It can change a solid material into liquid, or change liquid into gas.
- Taking heat out of food by chilling it or freezing it makes the food last longer.
- Heat travels in three ways – by conduction, convection and radiation.
- Metals are good conductors of heat.
- Insulating materials such as plastic are poor conductors of heat.

We use the Celsius and Fahrenheit temperature scales in our everyday lives, but scientists use a different temperature scale. Called the kelvin scale, it begins with 0K (zero degrees kelvin) at absolute zero. On this scale, water freezes at 273.16 degrees kelvin! The kelvin temperature scale was named after a famous scientist called Lord Kelvin.

▲ Foam plastic cups keep hot drinks hot because the cups are poor conductors of heat.

THE SCIENCE OF HEAT

If the coldest possible temperature is absolute zero, is there a maximum possible temperature, the hottest anything can possibly be? Well, there might be. Scientists aren't sure. One possibility is called the Planck Temperature. This is about 100 million million million million million degrees kelvin – or, 1 followed by 32 zeroes!

Glossary

absolute zero coldest possible temperature

absorb take in or soak up

atom basic building block of matter

bacteria microscopic single-cell organisms that can cause illness

bamboo type of grass with stiff, strong, hollow stems

conduction movement of heat or electrical energy through a material

conductor material that allows heat or electricity to pass through it easily

convection spread of heat from one place to another by movements of liquids and gases

crude oil oil that comes out of the ground; unprocessed oil, also called petroleum

dehydration drying out, the removal of water from something

drilling rig equipment for drilling an oil well

electromagnetic energy type of energy that travels through space in the form of electric and magnetic waves

energy ability to do work, measured in joules

evaporate change from liquid into vapour

foam substance containing lots of bubbles to make it lighter in weight or a better insulator

fuel material such as kerosene or coal containing energy that can be converted into heat energy

generator machine for producing electricity

heat type of energy arising from the vibrations of atoms

iceberg large block of ice floating in the sea

impermeable not allowing liquid or gas to pass through

kinetic energy movement energy

microwave electromagnetic energy wave from about 1 millimetre (one twenty-fifth of an inch) to 1 metre (39 inches) long

mineral substance, not made of animal or vegetable matter, needed by the human body

molecule group of atoms joined together

natural gas gas, mainly methane, found underground

nutrient food substance that provides nourishment

offshore in the sea

preserve make something, such as food, last longer before it decays or rots

radar system for finding far-away objects and working out how far away they are by sending out radio waves and receiving any reflections that bounce back

radiation energy waves or particles given out by something

refinery chemical factory that separates out the many different substances in crude oil

refrigerated cooled or chilled

temperature warmth or cold measured on a scale

texture surface roughness of something and how it feels

turbine drum or disc with blades sticking out all around it, like a propeller with lots of blades, that spins like a waterwheel to create kinetic energy

vitamin substance needed in small amounts for good health

Find out more

Books

Experiments with Heat and Energy (Cool Science), Lisa Magloff (Gareth Stevens Publishing, 2010)

Fossil Fuels (Sci-Hi), Eve Hartman (Raintree, 2010)

Heat (The Science Behind), Darlene R. Stille (Raintree, 2013)

Hot! Heat Energy (Energy Everywhere), Emma Carlson Berne (PowerKids Press, 2013)

Hot Stuff: The Science of Heat and Cold (Big Bang Science Experiments), Jay Hawkins (Windmill Books, 2013)

Secrets of Heat and Cold (Science Secrets), Carol Ballard (Franklin Watts, 2014)

Temperature (Measure It!), Casey Rand (Heinemann Library, 2011)

The Oil Industry (Development or Destruction?), Richard Spilsbury (Wayland, 2014)

Think Like a Scientist in the Kitchen (Science Explorer Junior), Matt Mullins (Cherry Lake Publishing, 2011)

Websites

http://www.bakeinfo.co.nz/Facts/Bread-making/Science-of-bread-making/Baking

On this website you can read about the science of breadmaking.

http://www.eia.gov/kids/energy.cfm?page=oil_home-basics

Here you can find out more about crude oil, how it formed, where it is found and how it is refined.

http://www.exploratorium.edu/cooking/bread/bread_science.html

This website has more information about breadmaking science.

http://foodquality.weebly.com/protein.html

On this website all about food, you can find out what protein is, which foods contain it and what happens to it when it is cooked.

http://scienceforkids.kidipede.com/chemistry/atoms/heat.htm

You can read all about heat on this website.

Places to visit

At-Bristol
Anchor Road, Harbourside, Bristol, BS1 5DB
This is another great science place to visit. It is one of the UK's biggest interactive science centres.
http://www.at-bristol.org.uk/

Glasgow Science Centre
50 Pacific Quay, Glasgow, G51 1EA
http://www.glasgowsciencecentre.org/

Science Museum
Exhibition Road, South Kensington, London, SW7 2DD
The Science Museum is a very good place to visit to find out about any science or technology, including heat. Look on their website for details of special events, shows, and exhibitions.
http://www.sciencemuseum.org.uk

Techniquest
Stuart Street, Cardiff, Wales, CF10 5BW
http://www.techniquest.org/

W5 (whowhatwherewhenwhy)
Belfast, Northern Ireland, BT3 9QQ
http://www.w5online.co.uk/

Further research

There is a lot more to learn about heat. Here are some ideas for topics to research.

- Did you know that Earth's centre is as hot as the surface of the Sun? Why do you think it is so hot?
- Do you think Earth has always been the same temperature? Was it cooler or hotter in the past?
- Why do you think California is warmer than Sweden?

Index